LEARNING CHILD BEHAVIORAL PSYCHOLOGY

JOHN LOK

Made with ♥ on the Notion Press Platform
www.notionpress.com

Contents

Foreword

Why does the child cry? What needs do general children cry? Is it only means that cry implies children feel unhappy or children have emotion problem? Does child cry represent the child hopes to do something, but the child feels difficult to do? Is child feels need to cry, his /her crying behavior may she / she learns easily after he /she crys? Can cry assist child learns more easily?

In my this book, I shall attempt to explain whether what childs wants when the child drys. Parents and teachers may learn whether the child crys, the child hopes what he / she feels need in order to improve learn ability or learning attitude more better in possible.

Prologue

Table of content

CHAPTER ONE

Factors cause child feels crying emotion need

Child crying behavior implies what the child need
In general, children cry when they are hungry, tried, uncomfortable, in pain, frustrated, angry. However, children cry less as they get older. However, child crys, whether his / her any behavior identifies the child feels special need? Reluctance or avoidance of tasks that require attention or concentration. Being easily distracted, forgetful and careless are also noticed. Excessive talking, out of seat behavior and difficulty with quiet play. All of these behavior can represent the child may feel special need in possible.
So, parents ought need to considerate whether what their child feels special need. For 1 to 5 year old child example, this age child always crys . One of the most frequent reasons children cry ius because they are overtired. Being unrested can lead to seem irrational behavior. So, enough sleeping time ought help this age group children suddenly cry. Their suddenly cry may due to they need attention.

Sometimes, children just need parent attention, and they can not or do not know how to ask, for it. If their parents have ruled out all other causes of crying, such as hugry, overstimulation and frustration, it might be time to ask parents themselves if their children just need some time with them.

There are the common type of special needs to children. such as physical muscular, dystrophy, multiple dystrophy, multiple scierosis, chronic asthma etc. developmental, down syndrome, autism, dyslexia, procsssing disorders. Behavioral / emotion, oppositional defiance disorder etc.

However, on learning difficulties aspect, some children feel need to cry. They may feel learning difficult problems. So, schools need have target special teaching strategies to deal with them, e.g. anxiety, hearing impairment, oppositional defiant disorder, visual impairment, nonverbal learning disabilities, language processing disorder, anditory processing disorder. All of these physical problems may influence some child feels to cry to aim to represent negative emotion feeling or learning difficult aspect.

So , children cry may bring some signs of learning disabilities, e.g. problem reading and / or writing problems with math, poor memory, problems saying attention, trouble following directions, problems staying organized. Are some chilfren lazy or learning disabled? The first way to determine whether or not your children are lazy or learning disabled is to see of your children are succeeding at school. If your children are succeeding , why both working hard? If this is your children, youe children may be avoiding more difficult work for fear that your children may fail. Also, when your children feel often forget what they learn, they may also often cry to represent theiur negative emotion. There are many reasons to explain children are forgetful, including stress and lack of sleep. Being hungry can also have a big impact. But sometimes when children have trouble remambering information, they may be a skill called working memory. So, these evidences may explain that a child crys, his /her crying behavior may imply that he /she feels learning difficulty. Parents and teachers ought treat a slow learner by these methods or learning attitudes as below:

Compensatory teaching, remedial teaching, instructional strategies for slow leaners, develop lessons that incoorporate students' interests, needs and experiences, frequent vary your instructional technique, incorporate individualized learning materials, audio and visual materials.

Hence, child crying behavior may represent he / she is one slow learner and the child feels problem of slow learning. So, the feeling problems of slow learning may cause the child needs to ary to represent his / her negative emotion. There are so many factors that could cause the process of slow learning . The slow learners have a short attention span with which they can not concentrate for long time. They have the problem of short memory and they do not remember what they learn. They get bored easily and develop no interest towards learning process.

On conclusion, children crying behavior implies what the child needs? Many psychological evidences prove that child crying behavior may identify the child feels special need. Every child is unique. Children have built own strengths and weaknesses. Their development progresses according to cetrtain sequences. It is natural that some children may excel in certain area, but have deficiencies in otehr areas. However, if children display marked problems or difficulties in one or more development areas. They may often cry to let their negative emotion feeling may be let to others to know. Their cry aim may hope others may help them to solve any one psychological problem, e.g. feeling difficulties to learn. So , the problem of feeling difficulty to learn may cause they feel unhappy or sad. Then, their negative emotion cause their crying behaviors. Hence, child crying behavior sources may come from school, family, society, and child's developmental conditions, e.g. they have problems in attention control, recent families conflict have upset them and affect their concentration in class, the noisy environment of the school easily distraqcts their attention, the child feels communication difficulties between teachers and parents, he /she feels that they are negligent to care their needs, the child dislikes to go to school to learn because he /she feels difficult to learn. Aoo of these factors may influence any one child feels to cry to represent his / her negative emotion on any loving aspects.

CHAPTER TWO

What learners crying behavioral reflection

Can child crying behavior represents learning need
Children crying behavior implies what the child needs, e.g. learning difficult or disliking learning negative emotion real feeling or other non learning negative emotion feeling more ? Many psychological evidences prove that child crying behavior may identify the child feels special need. Every child is unique. Children have built own strengths and weaknesses. Their development progresses according to cetrtain sequences. It is natural that some children may excel in certain area, but have deficiencies in otehr areas. However, if children display marked problems or difficulties in one or more development areas. They may often cry to let their negative emotion feeling may be let to others to know. Their cry aim may hope others may help them to solve any one psychological problem, e.g. feeling difficulties to learn. So , the problem of feeling difficulty to learn may cause they feel unhappy or sad. Then, their negative emotion cause their crying behaviors. Hence, child crying behavior sources may come from school, family, society, and child's developmental conditions, e.g. they have problems in attention control, recent families

conflict have upset them and affect their concentration in class, the noisy environment of the school easily distraqcts their attention, the child feels communication difficulties between teachers and parents, he /she feels that they are negligent to care their needs, the child dislikes to go to school to learn because he /she feels difficult to learn. Aoo of these factors may influence any one child feels to cry to represent his / her negative emotion on any loving aspects. Is crying considered a behavior? If child crying is to be considered a real self soothing behavior, then it should also result in mood improvements when crying alone, with no others present. In fact, crying is an important part of children's social- emotion development. Instead of demanding that they stop, create an emotionally safe classroom with patients, acceptance is concerned to children's learning need emotional performance to crying behavior.

The classroom is one of only a few primary places in which children can develop sense of self-communicate , and grow in relation to others. It brings this question: Is the child feels to raise learning need if he /she often crys in classroom suddenly? Children experience conflicts and growing pains that can be challenging for a teacher who is balancing instruction with individual learning and group dynamics.

In fact, when a child crys in classroom, his /her tears have many biological and psychological based that have been discovered through research as below:

Tear may reflect attachment styles, for example, individuals who are move comfortable expressing emotions tend to cry in ways that are considered typical and healthy to research by psychotherapist judith Kay Kelson, PHD. He explained that tear serves as an important communication tool, allowing research by psychologist and neuroscienist Robert R. Provine PHD. He explained that tears are an excrine process, and it had been suggested that they can relieve stress by expelling potentially harmful stress-induced chemicals from the body (refer to research by biochemist William H. Frey PHD). So, it seems that a pupil crys in classroom. His / her crying behavior may reflect that he /she feels that he /she wants teacher to teach him/her can get better understanding whether what the teacher is teaching easily or the pupil feels that the teacher needs to improve his /her teaching method.

However, if pupil individual tears are necessary to represent their learning feeling, why is crying in classroom so difficult to deal with? Because tears also bring up other people's care emotion (sadnessm frustration, disappointing etc.) and any teacher could fear whether conscious or not, that it increases emotional chaos for others, prticularly oneself. Teaching is a complex system with many moving parts, and a crying pupil could represent a system in collapse.

How to solve child crying behavior when he s/he feels difficult learning ? Children need space and time to experience the initial response of the emotion and feel if all the way through acceptance overrides demands. Demanding that students refrain from crying goes against their natural process of assimilating information . Rather, use teacher himself / herself own energy to accept core emotions as a basis for student's learning.

Being compassionate and open, listening with open and compassionate ears takes into account the complexity of tears and human experience. Create an emotionally safe classroom through discussion and brain-storming. Depending on the grade level, teachers can help students identify a range of feelings that may come up in reponse to different challenges, and express acceptance for them for teacher individual tolerance and empathy behavioral performance. Their teaching behaviors can let crying student to feel that they are real responsibility teachers. For example, when high school students understand the key components of executive functioning. They are better prepared to plan their time successfully. When they understand the difference between tasks that are urgent and those that are important, they are better prepared needs become more complex among high school students as their life roler evolve other their efforts to engage in goal-oriented behaviors become strained by navigating acedemics, extracurricular activities, socializing and part time jobs.

Can child crying behavior needs learning satisfaction

Too oiften, all of these student individual free learning time, it can influence their feeling whether they feel pressure or not pressure on learning aspect. So, when the student crys in classroom, his /her crying behavior may represent he s/he feels pressure to learn. So, teacher needs to consider how to solve his /her negative emotion on learning challenge.

In fact, pupil crying behavior and classroom management , they have close relationship. So, pupils crying behavior may imply that whether they can feel learning satisfaction or dissatisfaction. So, classroom discipline is a real problem may cause any student feels dissatisfactory main factor because when one classroom discipline is poor, the classroom students are often absent, or make noise to influence themselves learn in classroom. Then, dissatisfactory students to teacher teaching method or skill will be influenced to bring more dissatisfactory feeling. So, dissatisfactory students number may be increased, when the classroom discipline is often poor in this poor classroom learning environment. So, it seems that the main factor influences pupils often cry in classroom is due to the classroom discipline is poor to cause many pupils feel learning satisfaction. So, in long time poor classroom learning environment, they only choose to cry to represent their difficult learning emotion, they aim to complaint the teacher individual poor teaching performance to let him/ her to know.

Can child crying behavior aims to let teacher knows need to
improve education method

As above evidence indicates that in general, pupils‘ crying behavior may reflect that they feel dissatisfactory to their teacher individual teaching behavior in classroom. If it is true, whether in general pupils crying behavior can reflect that they hope their teachers need to improve their teaching method . I shall attempt to apply child's emotion psychological view to explain whether they have relationship between pupil crying behavior and improving teaching method need.

All observational study was conducted to examine teachers' emotional socialization strategies. Qualitative analysis of the data suggests that teachers can respond to children's emotional expressions with various strategies when they see their pupils cry in classroom suddenly. Teachers clearly expressed a preference for positive emotion through verbal reinforcement. They encouraged not only children's smiles, laughter and affection seeking behaviors, but also their empathy toward other children. Observations indicate that negative responses to children's emotional expressions imply that some teachers' emotional socialization practices need to be improved.

The implications of a teacher's emotional socialization practice factor, it may influence any student whether he /she needs the teacher to improve his /her teaching methods or skills, even some stidents may make crying behavior to imply their dissatisfactory to their teacher individual teaching method or skill or attitude. Hence, it is especially very important to conduct action research that enables cooperation with the researcher and the educators aiming to deeply analyze the impacts of the offered teacher training and how it should be and examing the actual pupil personal feeling learning dissatisfactory challenge, when they discovered theiry child students often cry suddenly in classroom.

I suggest that a teaching training practice may be used to solve student individual dissatisfactory learning feeling challenge. such as demonstration, videotaped examples, discussing and role playing and feedback about crying student participant program. All of these teaching methods may be suggested to attempted to solve crying student individual dissatisfactory learning need emotional challenge. So, it seems that it has close relationship between one sudden crying student whose crying behavior and his/her dissatisfactory learning need from the teacher individual teaching method.

www.ingramcontent.com/pod-product-compliance
Ingram Content Group UK Ltd.
Pitfield, Milton Keynes, MK11 3LW, UK
UKHW040014200726
13854UKWH00001B/198